Arm & Finger
Knitting

35 no-needle knits for the home and to wear

Laura Strutt

CICO BOOKS
LONDON NEW YORK

Published in 2015 by CICO Books
An imprint of Ryland Peters & Small Ltd

20–21 Jockey's Fields
-London WC1R 4BW

341 E 116th St
New York, NY 10029

www.rylandpeters.com

10 9 8 7 6 5 4 3 2 1

A CIP catalog record for this book is available from
the Library of Congress and the British Library.

ISBN: 978-1-78249-208-5

Printed in China

Editor: Emily Davies
Designer: Isobel Gillan
Photographer: Penny Wincer
Stylists: Isabel de Cordova, Kiki Tse

In-house designer: Fahema Khanam
Art director: Sally Powell
Production: Gordana Simakovic
Publishing manager: Penny Craig
Publisher: Cindy Richards

contents

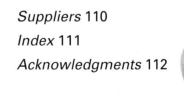

introduction

Modern yarn comes in all styles, colors, and sizes— so no wonder it seems to be getting more appealing by the day! Making your own garments, accessories, and pieces for your home is rewarding as a creative pastime and is also a great way to put your own individual stamp on your personal style and surroundings.

For many people, knitting seems like a tricky business, and some are put off by the perceived time-consuming aspect of hand-knitted projects. Having first learnt to knit as a child—with needles—I am always looking for new ways to create beautiful things for myself, as gifts, and for my home, using yarn.

Knitting without needles, using your arms or fingers, is fast becoming one of the most popular ways to create with yarn. Arm and finger knitting is quick, fun, and a highly creative way to transform skeins of colorful yarn into almost instant finished pieces. Arm knitting is far more free-form than standard knitting with needles; while you might be used to working with gauges, setting the correct tension, and working carefully with colorwork charts, this form of knitting is more organic in nature. While there are a number of techniques, stitches, and terms that will apply to both these forms, arm knitting creates a fabric that is much larger in scale compared to knitting with needles—even the most chunky needles— so the fabrics created behave in different ways. These projects are designed to give you an insight into the different techniques you can try; have a go, get inspired, and experiment with your own designs!

Whether you have knitted for years or are feeling tempted by the array of yarn on offer, now is the time to learn with this easy guide to no-needle knitting. With nothing more than a few balls of yarn and your own hands, you can create striking contemporary makes to wear, for your interiors, or to give as gifts.

Happy knitting!

Laura

tools and materials

Yarns

The majority of yarns that are used in arm knitting are chunky or super chunky yarns. As you're using your arms in place of needles these heavyweight yarns help to create a fabric that is not too lacy and flyaway.

You can work with two or more strands of the same—or different—yarns at the same time in order to create different effects in the finished knitted piece.

Finger knitting can be done with a wider range of yarns—from double knitting through to super chunky—depending on the density required on the finished piece.

Split-eye needle

When sewing together the projects or weaving in the loose ends, you might find that a split-eye needle (right) is much easier to use than trying to thread the eye of a standard tapestry needle with very chunky yarn. The hinged opening allows you to insert yarns into the eye and close it back up ready for stitching. You can also use your fingers to weave the yarns ends in too, if you prefer!

USEFUL TERMS & ABBREVIATIONS

Casting on: making the foundation stitches from which you will knit.

Binding (casting) off: securing the stitches when the work is complete, so that the knitting will not unravel.

Working yarn: this is the length of yarn that runs toward the ball, so called because it is the yarn that you are working with to form the stitches.

Yarn tail: this is the name given to the cut end of the yarn; the opposite strand to the working yarn.

K: knit

P: purl

K2tog: knit two stitches together to decrease

St(s): stitch(es)

KFB: knit into the front and back of the stitch to increase

arm knitting techniques

Knitting without needles is simple once you know how, but here are some tips to help you along. One of the things I love most about arm knitting is not only how quickly you can complete bold statement projects, but how quick it is to learn. Before you know it the fluid motions for creating the stitches will flow easily!

Long-tail casting on

The majority of arm knitting projects will use the long-tail method of casting on; this involves taking a length of yarn from the ball and using this to create the foundation stitches. The long-tail method will give a strong and sturdy base to the stitches from which you will be knitting.

1 The starting point of the foundation or cast-on stitches is to create a slip knot. Begin by drawing out a length of yarn from the ball; you'll need approximately 1–2 forearm lengths per ten stitches to be cast on.

2 With the length of yarn (the yarn tail) drawn from the ball, make a loop by taking the working yarn (the yarn on the side of the ball) over the yarn tail. Reach through the loop to take hold of the working yarn and draw it through, hold this section firmly while drawing up on both the yarn ends to fasten the slip knot into place.

3 Slide the slip knot over your right hand and onto your wrist, adjusting the yarn to make the slip knot sit snugly on the wrist. The two ends of the yarn will be hanging from your wrist, arrange them so that the yarn tail sits to the left-hand side and the working yarn sits to the right-hand side. With the yarns in this position you will be ready to cast on the stitches.

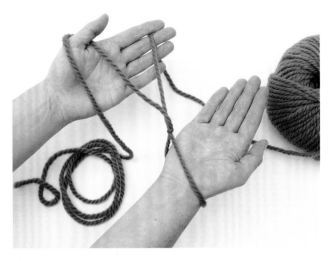

4 Pass the yarn tail over the palm of your left hand, looping over your thumb. The yarn tail will be the lower section of this loop and will sit closer to your wrist.

5 Pass your right hand under the lower loop on your palm and over the upper loop.

6 Take hold of the working yarn and draw your hand back through the loop over your left palm.

7 This loop will become the stitch. Once it has passed over the loop on your palm, slide it over your right hand and onto your wrist.

8 Draw the stitch to sit fairly snugly on your wrist by pulling on the yarn tail and the working yarn in turn.

9 Repeat these steps to create the required number of stitches, sliding the previous ones up your arm to make space.

STITCH HOLDER

The projects in the book are quick and easy to make—you can complete many of them in a couple of hours at the most. However, there might be times when you do need to stop partway through. As the knitting is carried on your arms, it is not as simple as knitting to the end of a row and stowing the project away safely. If you do need to stop knitting midway through a project, you can create your own arm knitting stitch holder with the use of a thin leather belt or even a length of chunky weight scrap yarn. Simply knit to the end of the row, hold the belt end in your hand and begin feeding the stitching onto the length of leather or yarn. Once all the stitches are held on the belt you can fasten the buckle or tie the yarn to hold them in place. To return the stitches to your arm, simple unfasten the belt buckle or untie the yarn knot and begin sliding the stitches back onto your arm ready to knit.

Knitting the first row

The stitches are knitted with the working yarn, the end attached to the ball or cone.
To avoid confusion, fold and knot the yarn tail left from casting on.

1 With your right hand pick up the working yarn from underneath, so that the yarn passes between your thumb and first finger, and hold securely in your right fist. Use your left hand to pick up the first stitch on your right arm.

2 Lift the stitch, pass it over your right hand, and drop it. The yarn held in your right hand will be drawn through to become the new stitch.

3 The new stitch needs to be rotated slightly before being placed onto your left arm, so the section of the stitch that lies over the front of your arm will lead directly back to the ball of yarn. This prevents the stitches looking twisted on the finished piece.

4 Adjust the stitch by pulling on the working yarn so that it sits snugly on your wrist. Repeat these steps to knit the remaining stitches from your right arm over to your left arm.

Knitting the second row

This row is worked exactly the same as the first row, the only difference being the direction in which you are knitting and passing the stitches. You will now be picking up the stitches from the left arm, and knitting them onto the right arm.

1 Begin by picking up the working yarn and passing it under your left thumb, so that it lies in the palm of your left hand, and hold securely in your fist.

2 With the right hand pick up the first stitch and bring it over your left hand, drawing the working yarn through the stitch as you do so.

4 Repeat to knit the remaining stitches on your left arm in the same manner. Following rows will follow the same instructions as for first and second rows, depending on whether you are knitting from the right arm to the left, or the left arm to the right. This will create stockinette (stocking) stitch (see below).

3 Insert the right hand into the front of the stitch, rotating the stitch so that the working yarn lays across the front of your arm, and slide onto your right wrist. Ease the working yarn to secure the stitch snugly to your wrist.

Binding (casting) off

Once you have knitted the required amount of rows, you will need to secure the stitches by binding (casting) off.

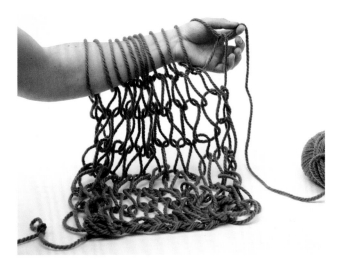

1 Finish a row with the stitches on your left arm and knit the first stitch onto your right arm.

2 Repeat to knit the second stitch in the same way. Use your left hand to pick up and lift the first stitch on your right arm over the second by bringing it over your right hand and dropping it. The first stitch will be secured in place by the second stitch.

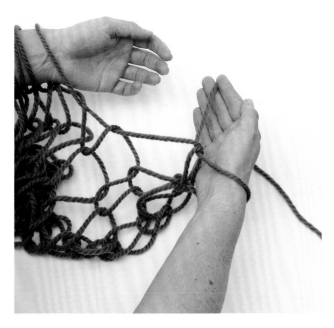

3 Knit the next stitch from your left arm onto your right, and repeat the process of passing the first stitch over the second on the right arm. Continue working across the row, knitting the next stitch, and then securing the one before it.

4 Once you have worked across the row there will be one remaining stitch on your right arm. Loosen off the stitch slightly before sliding it off your arm. Feed the working yarn through the stitch and slowly draw up to fasten off the final stitch. The remaining length of working yarn can be woven into the knitting, or can be used to secure any additional pieces.

Purl stitch

Purling the stitches gives more texture to the knitted fabric. Purl stitches are worked in the opposite direction to those of the knit stitch, by positioning the working yarn closer to your body. Drawing the yarn through from the front to the back of the stitch—rather than from the back to the front as with knitting a stitch—will result in a stitch that sits proud on the surface of the knitted fabric, creating a variation in texture. The sample (right) shows what several rows of purl stitch would look like, when using multiple strands of yarn.

1 Cast on the required number of stitches. With the working yarn positioned at the front of the work (closest to your body) make a loop in the yarn and draw it through the first stitch on your arm to make the stitch. The yarn is being drawn from the front to the back rather than the back to the front, as in the knit stitch.

2 Pass the stitch onto the other arm, positioning it so that the working yarn lies across the front of your arm to avoid twisting the stitches.

3 Repeat across the length of the row, working the yarn from the front to the back of each stitch to the end of the row. To purl stitches from the left arm onto the right arm, simply reverse the process, always keeping the yarn to the front of the work.

Increasing (kfb)

To shape a garment or object, you will need to increase and decrease the number of stitches. Increaasing is done by knitting the same stitch twice, once through the front (as a standard stitch) and then again through the back of the stitch to make the additional stitch.

1 Knit the stitch as usual, and place the new stitch on the other arm; do not release the knitted stitch from the previous arm. Rotate the arm and re-insert your hand though the back part of the stitch—this is the part of the stitch that lays on the back (furthest away from your body).

2 Draw the yarn though the stitch for the second time and place this new additional stitch onto the other arm. Make sure that the working yarn lies across the front of your arm, to avoid twisting the stitches.

Decreasing (k2tog)

Decreasing is done by knitting two stitches together, to make one stitch.

1 Insert the hand through the next two loops on the arm as if to knit, picking up the working yarn and drawing it though the two stitches at once, before placing the new stitch onto the other arm.

Seed (moss) stitch

A textured effect can be created by alternating between knit and purl stitches, in a pattern known as seed (moss) stitch. Start by knitting one stitch then purling the next, to the end of the row. On the second and subsequent rows, you will need to purl the stitches that were knitted on the previous row, and knit the stitches that were purled. The sample (right) shows moss stitch knitted with multiple strands of yarn.

In contrast, a rib stitch is created by knitting the stitches that were knitted on the previous row and purling the stitches that were purled on the previous row. This creates a striped effect of knit and purl stitches that run the length of the knitted fabric.

Working with multiple strands

Many patterns and arm knit designs will call for using a number of strands at the same time. This is achieved by drawing a length of working yarn from each of the balls of yarn, holding them together and threading them as a single strand to create the stitches.

1 To make the process easier, you can tie a small knot in the tails of the yarns to hold them together while you draw out the lengths for casting on.

2 When knitting, be sure that you have picked up each of the different strands of yarn as you work each stitch.

Cable stitch

A cable is created by slipping some of the stitches off your arm and holding them out of the knitting sequence, knitting some of the remaining stitches first, before returning the held stitches back to the arm and knitting them. By changing the order in which these stitches are knitted, a twist or cable is created in the knitted fabric, as in the Twisted Stitch Lap Blanket on page 40.

1 Cast on the required number of stitches, and work one row as directed in the pattern.

2 Knit as instructed until you come to the point where the cable will be created. For a six-stitch cable, slide the next three stitches from the left arm onto the right thumb without knitting them.

3 Knit the next three stitches from the left arm onto the right arm. You will need to transfer the held stitches back and forth from the right-hand thumb to the left hand in order to allow you to secure the knitted stitches onto the right arm.

4 Without twisting the stitches, return the three stitches held on the right-hand thumb over onto the left arm and knit to the end of the row.

5 Work more rows as directed by the pattern, knitting all the stitches. Repeat the cabling as directed by the pattern.

finger knitting techniques

Finger knitting is a quick and easy way to make a knitted strip using only your hands. By working the yarn over the fingers before dropping the stitches off the tips of the fingers, you can quickly and easily make long lengths of knitted cord and strips. You can use two, three, or four fingers for this technique.

Knitting with two fingers

Casting on two finger knitting

1 Place the tail end of the yarn in the palm of your left hand. Bring the working yarn over the back of the hand and round the index finger.

2 Pass the yarn between the index and middle fingers, and re-wrap between these two fingers to create a figure of eight between the fingers, with two strands on each finger. Position the working yarn at the center of the figure of eight in the palm of your hand.

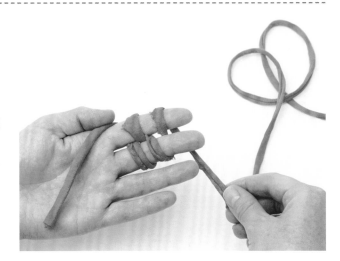

Working the stitches

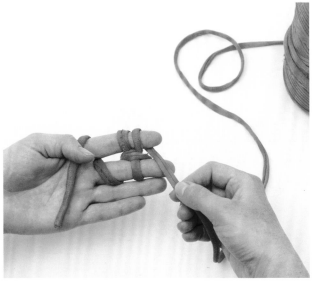

1 Starting with the index finger, bring the lower loop over the upper loop and drop it off the top of the finger. Repeat with the lower loop on the middle finger. This creates the first stitch.

2 Re-wrap the yarn in a figure of eight around the index then middle finger to create two more loops of yarn on each finger.

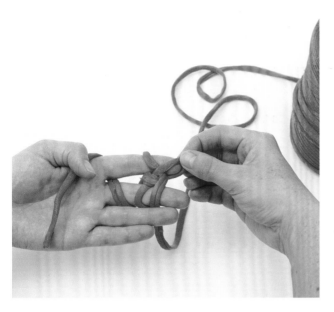

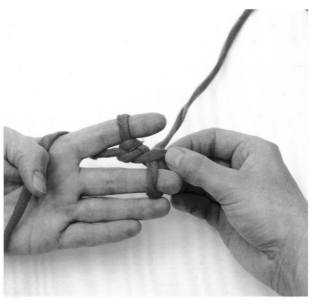

3 Starting with the index finger again, pass the lower loop of yarn over the upper loop and drop it off the tip of the finger.

4 Repeat to pass the lower loop on the second finger over the fingertip.

5 Pull gently on the length of finger knitting every few rows to neaten the stitches. Continue to desired length.

Fastening off two finger knitting

1 Once the desired length has been knitted, do not re-wrap the yarn around the fingers, leaving only one loop of yarn on each finger. Snip the yarn tail, leaving a minimum of 2 in. (5 cm).

2 Slide the fingers out of the loops and feed the yarn end through the loops.

3 Draw up the yarn end to tighten the loop and secure the finger knitting.

Knitting with three or four fingers

Chunkier lengths of knitted cord or strips can be created by finger knitting over three or four fingers, using the same technique as finger knitting with two fingers.

Working the stitches

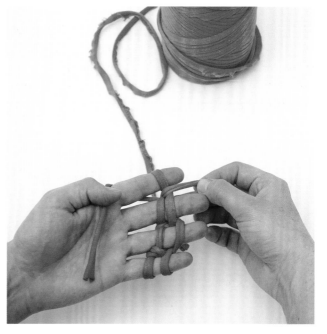

1 Rather than figure of eights, the yarn is woven from one side of the hand to the other and back, working between the chosen number of fingers. Repeat the weaving process until each finger has two loops around it.

2 Starting at the index finger, take the lower loop over the upper one and drop off the fingertip.

3 Repeat to work the stitches on each finger in turn. Continue in this manner until the desired length is created.

Fastening off three and four finger knitting

1 Fasten off the stitches by simply cutting the yarn end and feeding it through the stitches, then drawing it up tightly to secure the stitches.

finishing touches

These techniques will show you how to finish the projects in this book, or to add a professional touch to your own designs.

Weaving in ends

When you finish your arm knitting, you will have leftover yarn tails where you have joined in new lengths of yarn, and at the cast-on and bound-off (cast-off) edges of your work. Weaving these back through the work will secure the loose ends, and will also give a neat finish, without any stray pieces of yarn hanging from the project.

1 With the wrong side of the project uppermost, take one of the yarn ends and, following the pattern of the stitches, begin weaving it through the knitting for three to four stitches. If your project has used multiple strands of yarn, try weaving each one in separately—working along different sets of stitches—for a more discreet finish.

2 Once the ends have been woven through, work a small knot in the tail of the yarn around part of one of the stitches on the wrong side of the project. A small knot will hold this securely and will not be visible on the right side. Neatly snip away the excess yarn after the knot.

IDENTIFYING THE RIGHT SIDE AND THE WRONG SIDE

When working with only a knit stitch in arm knitting, there will be a distinct difference in the right side and the wrong side of the project, similar to when working in stockinette (stocking) stitch in hand knitting.

The right side will have a smooth flat surface and rows of V shaped stitches will be easy to identify.

The wrong side will have considerably more texture, created with rows of neat even bumps.

Seaming arm knitting

Sections can be joined together using mattress stitch, which is easy to work using just your fingers, or perhaps a split-eye needle if you prefer. If you have long yarn tails left attached to your projects you can use these to join the two pieces together, or you can simply cut a length of yarn and use that, weaving each end in securely once the seam has been created.

1 Place the two pieces to be joined together next to each other with right sides uppermost. Make sure that the knitted pieces are neatly aligned with the rows running horizontally. Working one stitch from each of the edges to be joined, identify the horizontal bars that make up the stitches—these are the sections through which the seams will be created.

2 Flatten out the side sections that will be joined and take the yarn tail from one piece and bring it over to the second piece. Pass the yarn through the knitting, drawing it under two horizontal bars made by the stitches, and bring it back up to the right side.

3 Bring the yarn over to the second piece and pass the yarn through to the wrong side, drawing it under two horizontal bars of stitches before bringing it to the surface. When the yarn is drawn up tightly the two sections will be brought together to create a neat and nearly invisible seam. Repeat in the same manner, working on each side in turn to join the two pieces together across the entire length of the seam.

4 Secure the ends and weave in before knotting and snipping away the excess yarns.

Finishing finger knitting

The process of weaving in the ends and seaming together pieces of finger knitting is done in the same manner as arm knitting—although you will be working on much smaller stitches.

Weaving in the ends

1 Weave the ends of the yarn back through the finger knitted section, before knotting and snipping away the excess.

Seaming together

1 Place the pieces to be joined with right sides together. Using a needle and yarn, or sewing thread, and working one stitch in from the outer edges, begin making small stitches through the horizontal bars on one side, then the next.

2 Draw up the yarn or thread tail to neaten the seam, before weaving in the yarn or thread end.

Making yarn substitutions

You could create all the projects featured in this book using the yarns that are listed within the text. However, because we all have our own unique sense of style, you might want to customize the projects shown by working with your own choice of yarns. There are a few things that you will need to consider when using different yarns for your projects. Use this guide to help you select suitable subsitute yarns for successful finished projects.

Every project includes details of the qualities of the yarns: the weight, the fiber content, and also the yardage (meterage) per ball. It is this information that will help you to select a different yarn to the one we have used.

Yarn color

Changing the color of the project is one of the simplest and easiest ways to alter the appearance of the design to suit your personal taste. In many cases you will simply be able to select the same yarn in an alternative shade. A number of these projects are made with a few different yarns being held together and knitted as one single strand. You can change to a more uniform look by working with multiple strands of just one of the yarns—you just have to ensure that you have the correct amount of yarn to complete the project.

Yarn weight and gauge (tension)

The majority of the projects in this book are created using chunky or super chunky weight yarns, particularly for the arm-knitted projects. The reason for this is that the large stitches would be very loose and open in lighter-weight yarns, creating a much more fluid fabric and a lacier finish.

If you want to create the project with a similar look to the one shown, you will need to select a yarn with a similar weight, which also knits to a similar gauge. While the projects don't include a set gauge due to the variations in arm and finger size, you should select a substitute yarn that has the same recommended gauge (you'll find this on the ball band or the manuracturer's website) as the suggested yarn, to ensure that the replacement yarn will knit up to roughly the same size as the one used in the project.

Any yarn that is lighter or heavier in weight, or has a very different suggested gauge, will change the finished appearance of the project quite dramatically.

Yardage (meterage)

This term refers to the length of yarn on a single ball, skein, or cone. The number of balls needed for each make is included on each of the projects, along with the average yardage (meterage) per ball. This will allow you to determine how many balls, skeins, or cones of a replacement yarn you will need to select in order to make the project. If the yardage (meterage) per ball is different, multiply the number of balls times the length per ball in the suggested yarn to get the total length needed, then divide this by the number of yards (meters) per ball in the substitute yarn, to get the number of balls needed in that yarn.

Fiber

The final aspect to consider when selecting a substitute is the fiber that the yarn is made from. Some of the projects in this book are worked using a fabric, or T-shirt yarn, while others are made using a wool blend—each gives a different finish to the knitted fabrics. If you want the finished piece to have the same qualities as the project in the book you will need to select a yarn made with the same or similar fiber content.

TIP

If you are buying a large volume of yarn you should not only check the ball band to ensure that all the balls are the same shade, but also be sure to check the dye lot number. This number will indicate the batch that the yarn has been dyed in, and selecting balls from the same dye lot will ensure that there is color consistency within your project.

making your own T-shirt yarn

Some of the projects use branded T-shirt yarns which are sold in large cones, but it is really easy to create your own! If you are making one of the larger arm-knitting projects, you will need to use a lot of T-shirts, so it might be better to create this yarn only for smaller makes, to be time- and cost-efficient.

Materials
- Jersey fabric T-shirts, preferably with no side seams, in the largest size possible
- Ruler
- Tailor's chalk
- Sharp dressmaking shears

1 Lay the T-shirt out on a flat surface, and smooth out any wrinkles. Using the ruler and tailor's chalk, begin by drawing a line at the base of the T-shirt just above the lower hem, and then a second line at the upper section of the T-shirt, directly under the armhole sections.

2 Using the dressmaking shears, cut along the two drawn lines to remove the upper and lower sections of the T-shirt. Discard these pieces.

3 With the cut edges on the right and left, fold the bottom half of the T-shirt piece upward, leaving a gap of 1 in. (2.5 cm) below the edge of the piece underneath, and aligning the two side sections.

4 With the ruler and chalk, mark out a series of lines at 1 in. (2.5 cm) intervals, running down from the top of the shorter, upper layer to the bottom (folded) edge.

5 With the dressmaking shears, cut along the lines to create neat strips, leaving the 1 in. (2.5 cm) of the lower layer at the top uncut.

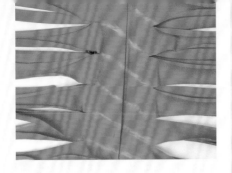

6 Open out the T-shirt and lay it out with the uncut edge running down the middle, like a backbone. Smooth out the fabric strips. Starting at the bottom of the fabric, begin neatly marking diagonal lines in tailor's chalk, from the top left of the first strip on the bottom, to the bottom left of the second strip on the top, and continue up the strips in this way.

7 Using the chalk lines as a guide, cut diagonally through the upper layer of fabric only, to create one long, continuous strip of fabric.

8 Shake the cut fabric out, then begin to gradually pull the strip through your hands, applying a little tension. The stretch in the fabric will cause the raw edges to curl up, to create the yarn.

Joining lengths of T-shirt yarn

If you have cut up a number of T-shirts into yarn and want to create a single ball, you could just tie the ends of the strips together, but for a neater finish, try either stitching or linking them together.

Stitching together

1 Create a small ¾ in. (1.5 cm) overlap, and either hand or machine stitch the two sections together.

Linking together

1 Slice a small ⅜ in. (1 cm) slit horizontally in one end of each of the two pieces of yarn to be joined, around ¾ in. (2 cm) from the ends.

2 Pass one uncut end of the second piece through the slit in the first piece, then feed the other end (without the slit) of the first piece through the slit in the second piece.

3 Pull on both ends so that the two pieces are linked tightly together a the point of the slits. Trim away the excess to neaten.

ARM KNITS

· · · · · · · · · · · · · · · ·

for the home

color pop scatter pillows

T-shirt or fabric yarns knit up to create a striking modern fabric—perfect for making an eye-catching set of scatter pillows. The simple construction of these pillows means that you can adapt them to any size you like, by simply increasing or decreasing the number of stitches and rows.

materials

- Hoooked Zpagetti fashion yarn: 1 cone—approx 131 yd (120 m)—per pillow in Pink, Mix Pink, and Lilac
- Pillow form, 13 in. (34 cm) square
- Large wooden buttons, nine (three per pillow)
- Yarn needle or split-eye needle

finished size

Finished cover is 14¼ in. (36 cm) square

time to make

You can make this project in an afternoon

TIP

When dividing the cones into separate balls of yarn, try to measure out each ball to the same number of arm lengths—this will help to ensure that each ball is of a similar length. Alternatively, place them on a pair of digital kitchen scales to check that the weight of each ball is the same.

color pop scatter pillow

Divide the cone of yarn into five balls of a similar length or weight (see Tip.)
With five strands held together, draw out two and a half arm lengths for the long-tail cast-on and cast on 7 sts.
Knit for 20 rows.
Bind (cast) off.

making up and finishing

Using the pillow form as a guide, fold the cast-on and bound-off (cast-off) edges in towards the center to overlap slightly. Use two strands of T-shirt or fabric yarn to neatly join the side seams with mattress stitch (see page 20.)

Using the yarn or split-eye needle, thread a length of T-shirt yarn and use to secure the buttons to the pillow, evenly spaced across the opening on the lower layer. Weave all yarn tails to finish before inserting the pillow form. To close the pillow, push the buttons through the fabric of the upper layer—no need for buttonholes.

MAKE IT YOURS

Each pillow uses one full cone of Hoooked Zpagetti, working with five strands at a time. You can change the appearance of the pillow by working with five different cones and making a set of multi-colored pillows.

comfy stool topper

Standard issue stools are commonplace in our homes, but there is no reason why these little essentials can't be made more attractive. Adding a small amount of padding and a neat fabric cover to the seat not only shows off the colorful arm knitted stitches, but also makes this sturdy wooden stool more comfortable too!

materials

- Debbie Bliss Paloma (60% baby alpaca, 40% merino wool) super chunky yarn:
  1 x 1¾ oz (50 g) skein—approx 71 yd (65 m) per skein—of shade 26 Lime (A)
  1 x 1¾ oz (50 g) skein—approx 71 yd (65 m) per skein—of shade 19 Dusky Rose (B)
- Foam pad, 1 in. (2.5 cm) thick x 15¼ in. (39 cm) square
- Cotton fabric, 1 yd (1 m)
- Spray adhesive
- Staple gun
- Stool

finished size

The stool topper is made to fit an Ikea Frosta stool with a seat diameter of 13½ in. (35 cm)

time to make

You can make this project in an afternoon

TIP

If you are able to remove the legs to create the custom stool pad, you will achieve a neater result when covering the stool.

comfy stool topper

Divide the skeins of yarn into two balls each to give four equal-sized balls.
With two strands of A and two strands of B held together (four strands in total), draw out four and a half arm lengths and cast on 12 sts.
Row 1: *K1, p1, repeat from * to end of row.
Row 2: *K1, p1, repeat from * to end of row.
Here you will be knitting the stitches that are purled and purling the stitches that have previously been knitted, this sets the pattern for seed (moss) stitch.
Continue in this pattern for a further six rows, eight rows in total.
Bind (cast) off knitwise.

making up and finishing

Draw around the seat of the stool onto the foam pad and trim to shape. Use the spray adhesive to secure the foam to the seat.

From the cotton fabric, cut a square that is 4½ in. (12 cm) larger than the seat of the stool. Remove the legs from the stool if possible.

Place the foam-covered stool top on the wrong side of the cotton and begin to fold the fabric in and around the underside of the stool. Work around the outer edge neatly making 1–1½ in. (2.5–4 cm) pleats and drawing the fabric in from the outer edge. Use a staple gun to secure into position.

Trim a circle of cotton fabric 1 in. (2.5 cm) smaller than the seat of the stool and use spray adhesive to cover the folded fabrics.

If you have removed the legs to cover the seat top, secure them back on now.

Place the covered stool top onto the knitted fabric. Begin to neatly fold the knitting over the stool, by drawing the two cast-on and two bound-off (cast-off) corners into the center. Use the yarn tails to weave through the point where they join at the center and secure to the stool; knot securely before trimming the yarn tails. For added security of the knitted panel, you can add in a couple of discreet staples to the underside of the stool to hold the knitted section in place.

TIP

Purl stitches require the yarn to be passed to the back of the work (closest to your body) before making each stitch (see page 12.) Ensure that the working yarn (that leads back to the balls of yarn) is over the front section of your arm on the completed stitch to prevent the stitches from becoming twisted.

MAKE IT YOURS

This stool topper can be made to custom-fit any stool. Simply measure the stool top and ensure that the knitted fabric is 4 in. (10 cm) larger than the stool top the entire way around in order for it to be large enough to cover it.

cozy striped throw

Knitting a large throw for your bed or couch would ordinarily be a labor-intensive project that you'd need to dedicate a number of hours to working on. By using a selection of chunky yarns and arm knitting, you can create a colorful throw for your home in just an afternoon.

materials

- Lion Brand Homespun (98% acrylic, 2% polyester) chunky yarn: 3 x 6 oz (170 g) balls—approx 185 yd (169 m) per ball—of shade 339 Apple Green (A)

- Lion Brand Hometown USA (100% acrylic) super chunky yarn: 2 x 5 oz (142 g) balls—approx 81 yd (74 m) per ball—of shade 172 Oklahoma City (B)

- Lion Brand Homespun Thick & Quick (88% acrylic, 12% polyester) super chunky yarn: 3 x 8 oz (227 g) balls—approx 160 yd (146 m) per ball—of shade 437 Dove (C)

- Split-eye needle

finished size

The completed throw measures approximately 63 x 45½ in. (160 x 116 cm) unstretched

time to make

You can make this project in under two hours

cozy striped throw

With three stands of A and two strands of B held together (five strands in total), draw out 15 arm lengths to create the long tail for casting on, and cast on 30 sts.
Knit three rows in A and B.
Rows 4–9: Knot three strands of C together and join in C at the start of the next row. Knit in C for six rows.
Rows 10–12: Change to A and B (five strands together), knit 3 rows.
Rows 13–18: Change to C (three strands), knit 6 rows.
Rows 19–21: Change to A and B (five strands together), knit 3 rows.
Rows 22–27: Change to C (three strands), knit 6 rows.
Rows 28–30: Change to A and B (five strands together), knit 3 rows.
Bind (cast) off in A and B.

making up and finishing

Start at the cast-on edge and weave in the yarn ends using the split-eye needle, knotting each strand separately for a neat finish. Work along the two sides of the throw in turn, weaving in and securing the ends with small discreet knots to finish.

bolster pillow

This sweet covered pillow looks great on couches or guest beds, is quick and easy to make and can be customized to suit any size bolster pillow form.

materials

- Lion Brand Homespun (98% acrylic, 2% polyester) chunky yarn: 1 x 6 oz (170 g) ball—approx 185 yd (169 m) per ball—of shade 416 Coral Reef
- Bolster pillow form, 17 in. long x 6 in. diameter (43 x 15 cm)
- Double-faced satin ribbon, cream 41 in. (104 cm)

finished size

Cover is approximately 28 in. wide x 25 in. deep (71 x 63 cm)

time to make

You can make this project in one hour

TIP

If you want a more textured finish, seam the knitted strip with the right sides innermost to display the more textured, ridged surface on the outside of the project.

bolster pillow

Divide the yarn into six equal balls. With six strands held together, draw out four arm lengths and cast on 12 sts.
Knit 12 rows.
Bind (cast) off.

making up and finishing

With the right side of the knitting outermost, join the cast-on and the bound-off (cast-off) edge using mattress stitch (see page 20.) Cut the ribbon in half and snip neat swallow tails into all the ends to prevent fraying. At each end, weave the ribbon through the stitches, two stitches in from each edge. Insert the bolster pillow form, and pull the ribbons to gather and secure the cover in place. Tie in neat bows.

MAKE IT YOURS

This cover has been created to fit the Ikea Lisel bolster pillow. You can make the cover larger or smaller by simply increasing or decreasing the number of stitches cast on and the number of rows worked, to suit the dimensions of your own pillow form.

seamed square blanket

Make your own patchwork effect blanket by joining together squares of arm knitting to create a simple, yet striking seamed square blanket.

materials

- Lion Brand Wool-Ease Thick & Quick (80% acrylic, 20% wool) super chunky yarn:
  2 x 6 oz (170 g) balls—approx 106 yd (80 m) per ball—each of shade 105 Glacier (A), shade 099 Fisherman (B), and shade 106 sky Blue (C)

- Lion Brand Wool-Ease Thick & Quick Metallics (79% acrylic, 20% wool, 1% metallic polyester) super chunky yarn:
  2 x 6 oz (170 g) balls—approx 92 yd (84 m) per ball—of shade 307 Mystical (D)

finished size

Approximate unstretched size: width 40 in. (102 cm), length 55 in. (140 cm)

time to make

You can make this project in an afternoon

TIP
To ensure that the seams are not too bulky on the finished blanket, try seaming with only two of the four strands used in the knitted square for a more discreet finish.

seamed square blanket

Square 1 (make 2)
With two strands of A and two strands of B held together (four strands in total), draw out four arm lengths for the long-tail cast-on, and cast on 15 sts.
Knit for 12 rows.
Bind (cast) off.

Square 2 (make 2)
With two strands of C and two strands of D held together (four strands in total), draw out four arm lengths for the long-tail cast-on, and cast on 15 sts.
Knit for 12 rows.
Bind (cast) off.

making up and finishing

Lay out the squares into two rows of two, positioning the matching squares diagonally opposite each other.
 Using the yarn tails, join the upper two squares together along the vertical center seam with mattress stitch. Fasten the yarn ends securely. Repeat to join the lower two squares in the same manner. Use the yarn tails to work along the horizontal center seams and fasten off securely. Weave in the ends neatly to finish.

two-tone tote

Ditch those plastic bags in favor of an arm-knitted tote and carry your groceries in style with this easy-make two-tone shopping bag.

materials

- Katia Cotton Cord (100% cotton) super chunky yarn: 2 x 3½ oz (100 g) balls—approx 55 yd (50 m) per ball—of shade 59 (A)
- Katia Cotton Cord (100% cotton) super chunky yarn: 2 x 3½ oz (100 g) balls—approx 55 yd (50 m) per ball—of shade 63 (B)

finished size

Approximate length: 33 in. (84 cm) including strap
Approximate width (at base of bag): 19½ in. (50 cm)

time to make

You can make this project in under an hour

TIP

When working with four strands of yarn held together, as in this pattern, rather than re-balling the yarns into separate balls, you can draw out the other end of yarn from the center of the ball and knit from both ends of the yarn ball at the same time.

two-tone tote

Side

With four strands of A held together, draw out three arm lengths for the long-tail cast-on and cast on 10 sts.

Rows 1–4: Knit all sts.
Row 5: K2tog (see page 13), knit to end. (9 sts)
Row 6: Knit to last 2 sts, k2tog. (8 sts)
Row 7: K2tog, knit to end. (7 sts)
Row 8: Knit to last 2 sts, k2tog. (6 sts)
Row 9: K2tog, knit to end. (5 sts)
Row 10: Knit to last 2 sts, k2tog. (4 sts)
Knit six rows.
Bind (cast) off.
Repeat to make second side in B.

making up and finishing

With right sides uppermost, join the two short ends of the bag to form the upper section of the strap using mattress stitch (see page 20.) Weave in the ends. Using the yarn tails, join the first four rows on each side for the side seams, and then the base seam, using mattress stitch (see page 20.) Weave in ends to finish.

MAKE IT YOURS

This mesh shopper bag is created with one color for each side, you can create the bag in a single shade by simply using four balls of the same yarn. Or, change up the look by working with two strands of each color on each side.

twisted stitch lap blanket

Snuggle up in this textured arm knit lap blanket, featuring a cable knitting technique to create a dramatic textured design that's so simple to knit.

materials

* Rowan Big Wool (100% merino wool) chunky yarn:
8 x 3½ oz (100 g) balls—approx 87 yd (80 m) per ball—of shade 051 Burnt Orange

finished size

Approximate size: 40 in. (102 cm) wide, 60 in. (153 cm) long

time to make

You can make this project in three hours

MAKE IT YOURS

Create a wider blanket by doubling the number of stitches cast on and repeating the pattern twice over each row. Be sure to increase the yarn amounts accordingly.

twisted stitch lap blanket

With four strands of yarn held together, draw out five and a half arm lengths and cast on 20 sts.

Row 1: K2, p16, k2.

Row 2: K2, p4. This will create the border. To make the twisted (cable) stitch (see also page 15), slide the next 4 sts from the left arm onto the right thumb without knitting them. Knit the next 4 sts from the left arm onto the right arm, working them behind the sts held on the thumb. You will need to transfer the held sts back and forth from the right-hand thumb to the left-hand thumb in order to allow you to secure the knitted sts onto the right arm. Without twisting the sts, return the 4 sts held on the right-hand thumb over onto the left arm and knit them. P4 and knit remaining 2 sts.

Row 3: K2, p4, k8, p4, k2.

Rows 2 and 3 create the twisted stitch pattern. Repeat these two rows 13 times more.

Next row: As Row 2.

Next row: K2, p16, k2.

Bind (cast) off.

making up and finishing

Weave in the yarn tails neatly to finish.

TIP

Be careful when you return the held stitches back to the working arm to ensure that you don't twist the stitches before you work them.

pom pom lampshade cover

Update a simple table lamp with a fun arm-knitted lampshade cover accented with pom pom trimmings.

materials

- Katia Big Ribbon (50% cotton, 50% polyester) fashion bulky yarn: 1 x 7 oz (200 g) ball—approx 77 yd (72 m) per ball—of shade 22
- Pom pom trimming, 25½ in. (65 cm)
- Table lamp with lampshade (such as Ikea Lampan)
- Superglue or hot glue gun

finished size

To fit a shade of approximate diameter 7½ in. (19 cm)

time to make

You can make this project in an afternoon

pom pom lampshade cover

Draw out three arm lengths and cast on 7 sts.
Knit 10 rows.
Bind (cast) off.

making up and finishing

Use the yarn ends to join the cast-on and bound-off (cast-off) edges together using mattress stitch (see page 20.) With the superglue or hot glue gun, secure the pom pom trimming around the lower edge of the lampshade, allowing the pom poms to hang below the base of the shade. Slide the knitted cover over the lampshade and secure in place with a few discreet dabs of glue to finish.

MAKE IT YOURS

You can create this lampshade cover to suit any table or standard lampshade. To increase the size simply increase the number of stitches cast on, and the number of rows worked.

TIP

When adding a knitted covering to lampshades, ensure that the yarn is not in direct contact with the bulb to prevent fire risk.

seed stitch throw

Alternating between knit and purl when arm knitting is a great way to add texture to your makes. This cuddly throw in seed (moss) stitch can easily be made in a few hours, and will look great on your bed or a favorite chair.

materials

- Lion Brand Hometown USA (100% acrylic) super chunky yarn: 6 x 4 oz (113 g) balls—approx 64 yd (59 m) per ball—of shade 213 Cheyenne Wild Iris (A)

- Lion Brand Homespun Thick & Quick (88% acrylic, 12% polyester) super chunky yarn: 3 x 8 oz (227 g) balls—approx 160 yd (146 m) per ball—of shade 437 Dove (B)

finished size

Approximate unstretched size: length 70 in. (178 cm), width 42 in. (106.5 cm)

time to make

You can make this project in two hours

MAKE IT YOURS

If you feel like taking on a more creative challenge, try working in stripes of different colored yarns in the same weight, alternating every few rows.

seed stitch throw

With two strands of A and one strand of B held together (three strands in total), draw out six arm lengths for the long-tail cast-on and cast on 22 sts.

Row 1: K1, p1. Repeat to end of row.

This pattern will create seed (moss) stitch. Continue working in this pattern for a further 33 rows—or until the work measures 69 in. (172.5 cm).

Bind (cast) off.

making up and finishing

Weave in the yarn tails on the cast-on and bound-off (cast-off) edges neatly to finish.

TIP

To keep track of whether you need to knit or purl the stitch you are working on, simply look at whether it was knitted or purled on the previous row—if it was a knit stitch, work a purl and if it was a purl stitch work a knit stitch.

tea cozy

Add a pretty flourish to the tea table with this sweet arm-knitted tea cozy!

materials

- Sirdar Kiko (51% wool, 49% acrylic) super chunky yarn: 2 x 1¾ oz (50 g) balls—approx 44 yd (40 m) per ball—of shade 410 Duffle
- Double-faced satin ribbon, silver gray, 30 in. (76 cm)

finished size

Approximate size: fits a standard 6-cup tea pot

time to make

You can make this project in under an hour

TIP

Dividing the yarn into three separate balls before you begin will make working on this project even quicker and easier.

tea cozy

With three strands of yarn held together, draw out one arm length for the long-tail cast-on and cast on 5 sts.
Knit 5 rows.
Bind (cast) off.
Make the second side in the same manner.

making up and finishing

Place the two pieces together with the wrong sides facing. At each side join two of the lower stitches using mattress stitch (see page 20.) Weave in the yarn ends and fasten off. Join one stitch at each of the side seams at the top of the tea cozy; this will leave a gap along each side seam through which to pass the spout and handle of the tea pot. Weave in the yarn ends and fasten off.

Weave the length of ribbon through the knitted stitches underneath the bound-off (cast-off) edge. Draw the ribbon in to gather the top of the tea cozy and secure in place with a bow. Trim the ends of the ribbon into a point to finish.

MAKE IT YOURS

Swap the satin ribbon for a piece of lace for a vintage-style finish!

woven pillow

The loose gauge of arm knitting makes the perfect canvas for interweaving with lengths of finger knitting. Use contrasting shades to thread in and out of the knitted fabric, and create a cozy and colorful pillow.

materials

- Lion Brand Hometown USA (100% acrylic) super chunky yarn:
  2 x 5 oz (142 g) balls—approx 81 yd (74 m) per ball—of shade 107 Charlotte Blue (A)
  1 x 5 oz (142 g) ball—approx 81 yd (74 m)—in each of shade 157 Daytona Lemon (B) and shade 144 Seattle Sea Mist (C)

- Pillow form, 15 in. (38 cm) square

finished size

Approximate size of cover: 16 in. (40 cm) square

time to make

You can make this project in under three hours

woven pillow

Pillow cover

With four strands of A held together, draw out two and a half arm lengths for the long-tail cast-on and cast on 9 sts.
Row 1: Knit all sts.
Repeat Row 1, 17 times more—or until the knitted strip is long enough to wrap around the pillow form.
Bind (cast) off.

Finger knitted accents

With B, finger knit over four fingers (see page 18) until the knitted length measures 36 in. (91.5 cm). Fasten off.
Repeat to create three more finger-knitted strips in B.
Also on four fingers, create three finger knitted strips in C.
In total there will be four 36 in. (91.5 cm) lengths in B and three 36 in. (91.5 cm) lengths in C.

making up and finishing

Fold the arm-knitted strip around the pillow form and use the yarn tails to seam along the two sides and base openings using mattress stitch (see page 20.) Weave the yarn tails in neatly to finish.

Starting at the bottom of the front of the pillow, begin weaving one of the B finger-knitted strips across the width, taking the strip over one stitch then under the next. Turn the pillow and repeat the weaving on the back following the same pattern. Join the two ends of the finger-knitted strip together using the yarn tails.

Working into the row of arm knitting directly above, begin weaving a C finger-knitted strip through the cover. Pass the strip over the knitted stitches the finger knitting passed under on the previous row, and under the stitches that the finger knitting passed over on the previous row, so alternating overs and unders from the first row. Turn the pillow and continue weaving on the back, and join the two ends together using the yarn tails.

Repeat in this pattern alternating between colors and stitches from the row previous until the entire pillow is covered.

TIP

To work with four strands of yarn you can either divide the ball into four equal weight balls, or work from both ends of two balls at the same time. Release the yarn tail that lies on the outside of the ball and place to one side, then insert your fingers into the center of the balls, find the other yarn tail, and draw it out.

MAKE IT YOURS

You can make this pillow to fit any size of pillow form by simply increasing or decreasing the number of stitches cast on, and the number of rows that are worked. Every few rows, hold the knitted strip against the pillow form to check the sizing and determine how many more rows to work. If you make it bigger, you will need additional finger-knitted strips.

travel blanket

This simple blanket features a handy pocket into which the whole thing can be folded and stowed away. It also doubles up as a comfy pillow—ideal for travel!

materials

- Sirdar Faroe (100% merino wool) super chunky yarn:
  6 x 1¾ oz (50 g) balls—approx 47 yd (43 m) per ball—of shade 0398 Meadow (A)

- Rowan Big Wool (100% merino wool) chunky yarn:
  4 x 3½ oz (100 g) balls—approx 87 yd (80 m) per ball—of shade 061 Concrete (B)

finished size

Approximate size: 50 in. long x 40 in. wide (127 cm x 101.5 cm)

time to make

You can make this project in three hours

TIP

Double check the size of the pocket by folding the two sides of the blanket into the center then folding in half—the pocket needs to be large enough to cover this surface area. To form a pillow, fold the side sections of the blanket in toward the middle and fold in half before tucking inside the pocket.

travel blanket

Blanket

With two strands of A and two strands of B held together (four strands in total), draw out five arm lengths for the long-tail cast-on, and cast on 20 sts.
Knit 24 rows.
Bind (cast) off.

Pocket

With two strands of B, draw out three arm lengths for the long-tail cast-on and cast on 15 sts.
Knit 9 rows.
Bind (cast) off.

making up and finishing

With the blanket wrong side uppermost, place the pocket section on top with the wrong side also uppermost. Align the cast-on edge of the pocket with the cast-on edge of the blanket, centering the pocket on this lower section of the blanket. Using the yarn tails, sew around the two sides and the base of the pocket to attach this to the blanket. Leave the upper section (that points to the center of the blanket) of the pocket unstitched.

Weave in all the yarn tails to finish.

MAKE IT YOURS

Upsize this blanket by casting on more stitches and working more rows—but remember to increase the size of the pocket to accommodate a larger blanket, and allow extra yarn.

ARM KNITS

· · · · · · · · · · · · ·

to wear

TIP

When seaming the short
ends together, be sure to lay each
of the sections to be joined smooth
on a flat surface. This will help you
to see the stitches through which
to pass the yarn to make the
mattress stitches for a neat and
discreet join.

infinity scarf

Create a cozy statement accessory fast—knit it today and wear it tonight! Teaming two styles of yarn makes for a wonderful and unique finish, and the shorter ends are seamed together to create a continuous loop of knitting that can be worn simply draped around the neck, or doubled up for a chunkier look.

materials

- Rowan Big Wool (100% merino wool) super chunky yarn:
  2 x 3½ oz (100 g) balls—approx 87 yd (80 m)—per ball of shade 054 Vert (A)

- Rowan Thick'n'Thin (100% wool) super chunky yarn:
  2 x 1¾ oz (50 g) balls—approx 54 yd (50 m) per ball—of shade 00962 Basalt (B)

- Split-eye needle

finished size

Scarf length is approximately 47 in. (120 cm) before seaming

time to make

You can make this project in under an hour

MAKE IT YOURS

Create a longer loop for your infinity scarf by using more balls of yarn, and continuing to knit to the desired length. Or knit with four strands of the same yarn to create a simpler finish to your knitted accessory.

infinity scarf

With two strands of A and two strands of B held together (four strands in total), draw out two arm lengths of all four strands for long-tail cast-on.
Cast on 8 sts in A and B (four strands).
Knit 27 rows in A and B (four strands).
Bind (cast) off.

making up and finishing

Use the yarn tails to join the two shorter ends together with mattress stitch (see page 20) to create the loop of the infinity scarf, being careful not to twist the strip of knitting.
Weave in the yarns tails to finish.

t-shirt yarn bolero

This colorful cover-up is quick and easy to make, and combines both knit and purl arm knitting stitches for added texture—perfect to slip over a summer dress.

materials

- We Are Knitters Fabric Yarn (100% recycled fabric yarn) worsted yarn: 1 x 14 oz (400 g) ball of shade Turquoise

finished size

Approximate sizing:
Small—to fit US 2–4 (UK 6–8)
Medium—to fit US 6–8 (UK 10–12)
Large—to fit US 10–12 (UK 14–16)

time to make

You can make this project in under two hours

t-shirt yarn bolero

Holding the yarn double, draw out four (**five**, six) arm lengths and cast on 12 (**14**, 16) sts.
Row 1: Purl all sts.
Row 2: Purl all sts.
Row 3: P2, k8 (**k10**, k12), p2.
Repeat Row 3 seven (**nine**, eleven) more times.
Next two rows: Purl all sts.
Bind (cast) off.

making up and finishing

With the wrong side of the knitting uppermost, fold in half along the length, aligning the two longer edges. Using mattress stitch (see page 20) and the yarn tails, join the sleeve sections together for three rows along each side. Weave in all loose ends to finish.

TIP

The instructions for the different sizes are shown in ascending order: Small (**Medium**, **Large**). Where there is only one instruction, this applies to all sizes. You can adjust the size further simply by casting on more or fewer stitches, and working more or fewer rows.

MAKE IT YOURS

Team the fabric T-shirt yarn with a soft and fluffy
mohair yarn in a complementary color for a more
feminine finish to the bolero.
To make your own T-shirt yarn, see page 23.

hand-warmer muff

Beat the chill with this fun retro hand-warming muff, working with fashion and fun fur yarns to create a striking accessory.

materials

- Lion Brand Imagine (40% acrylic, 30% wool, 30% nylon) super chunky yarn:
  3 x 1½ oz (40 g) balls—approx 8 yd (7 m) per ball—of shade 314 Purple Haze (A)

- Lion Brand Homespun Thick & Quick (88% acrylic, 12% polyester) super chunky yarn:
  1 x 8 oz (227 g) ball—approx 160 yd (146 m) per ball—of shade 437 Dove (B)

- Lion Brand Fun Fur (100% polyester) chunky yarn:
  1 x 1¾ oz (50 g) ball—approx 63 yd (58 m) per ball—of shade 98 Ivory (C)

finished size

Approximate size: 10 in. (25 cm) wide

time to make

You can make this project in an afternoon

> **MAKE IT YOURS**
> For a more subtle finish, replace the fun fur with a second yarn in a chunky weight.

arm knit muff

Muff

With A, draw out four arm lengths and cast on 8 sts.
Knit 9 rows.
Bind (cast) off.
The yarn tail will be approx. 100 in. (245 cm). Do not cut this as it will be used for seaming, and making the neck strap.

Lining

With two strands of B and two strands of C held together (four strands in total), draw out six arm lengths for the long-tail cast-on and cast on 10 sts.
Knit 8 rows.
Bind (cast) off.

making up and finishing

Place the outer muff and the lining together with wrong sides facing. Use the yarn tails from the lining to join the lining to the outer muff section at both of the short ends in turn. Use the long length of yarn tail from the outer section of the muff to join the seam along the length of the muff using mattress stitch (see page 20), being sure to secure both the lining and the muff outer in the seam. The lining section will roll outward to create fur-lined openings at both of the short ends.

Create the neck strap by folding the remaining length of yarn tail into three and neatly braiding (plaiting.) Knot it on the opposite side of the muff to secure the neck strap in place to finish.

TIP

Be sure not to get in a tangle when knitting with fun fur by dividing the ball into two separate, equal balls before beginning.

raspberry ripple shawl

Working with a simple decrease created by knitting two stitches together, you are able to change the shape of a piece of arm knitting. Here, even decreases are worked throughout the length of the projects, at the start and end of each row, to taper the knitting down to a point and create a triangular shawl.

materials

- Katia Zanzibar (100% acrylic) super bulky yarn:
  4 x 3½ oz (100 g) balls—approx 55 yd (50 m) per ball—of shade 0084

- Split-eye needle

finished size

Approximately 59 in. (150 cm) across the cast-on (upper neck) edge

time to make

You can make this project in under an hour

TIP

To create a really neat finish when weaving in the ends, it is possible to unravel the chain stitch effect of the Katia Zanzibar yarn and work with the much smaller single strands to make small, almost invisible knots to secure the ends.

raspberry ripple shawl

Working with four strands held as one, draw out ten arm lengths to create the long-tail cast-on.

Cast on 24 sts.

Row 1: Knit all sts. (24 sts)

Row 2: K2tog (see page 13), knit to last 2 sts, k2tog. (22 sts)

Row 3: K2tog, knit to last 2 sts, k2tog. (20 sts)

Row 4: K2tog, knit to last 2 sts, k2tog. (18 sts)

Row 5: K2tog, knit to last 2 sts, k2tog. (16 sts)

Row 6: K2tog, knit to last 2 sts, k2tog. (14 sts)

Row 7: K2tog, knit to last 2 sts, k2tog. (12 sts)

Row 8: K2tog, knit to last 2 sts, k2tog. (10 sts)

Row 9: K2tog, knit to last 2 sts, k2tog. (8 sts)

Row 10: K2tog, knit to last 2 sts, k2tog. (6 sts)

Row 11: K2tog, knit to last 2 sts, k2tog. (4 sts)

Row 12: K2tog, k2tog. (2 sts)

Row 13: K2tog. (1 st)

Bind (cast) off by feeding the tail of the yarn through the stitch and drawing up to secure.

making up and finishing

Weave in all loose ends to finish the shawl.

MAKE IT YOURS

Adding a decorative shawl pin is a great way to secure this shawl around your shoulders. To make a larger shawl, increase the size by adding in two or four more balls of yarn and starting with a greater number of cast-on stitches. Work with an even number of cast-on stitches, and use the same decrease pattern as set in the pattern.

simple wrap gilet

This stylish gilet is made with the simplest of construction, meaning that even the most novice arm knitters will be able to create their own garment in no time!

materials

- Rowan Big Wool (100% merino wool) super chunky yarn: 5 (**6**, 7) x 3½ oz (100 g) balls— approx 87 yd (80 m) per ball—of shade 061 Concrete
- Shawl pin (optional)

finished size

Approximate sizing:
Small—to fit US 2–4 (UK 6–8)
Medium—to fit US 6–8 (UK 10–12)
Large—to fit US 10–12 (UK 14–16)

time to make

You can make this project in an afternoon

TIP

The instructions for the different sizes are shown in ascending order: Small (**Medium**, Large). Where there is only one instruction, this applies to all sizes.

simple wrap gilet

Back Panel

With four strands of the yarn held together, draw out four (**five**, six) arm lengths for the long-tail cast-on and cast on 7 (**9**, 11) sts.
Knit 16 (**18**, 20) rows.
Bind (cast) off.

Side Panel (make 2)

With four strands of the yarn held together, draw out one and a half (**two**, two and a half) arm lengths for the long-tail cast-on and cast on 3 (**5**, 7) sts.
Knit 16 (**18**, 20) rows.
Bind (cast) off.

making up and finishing

Working on each side in turn, place the back and side panels to be joined with the right sides uppermost. Work in mattress stitch (see page 20) to join 12 in. (**12½ in.**, 13 in.)/31 cm (**32 cm**, 33 cm) from the cast-on edge upward to create the lower side seam. Make a second seam measuring 9 in. (**9½ in.**, 10 in.)/23 cm, (**24 cm**, 25 cm) from the bound-off (cast-off) edge downward to create the upper side/shoulder seam. Repeat to join the second side panel to the back panel on the other side. Weave in all yarn ends to finish.

MAKE IT YOURS

If you want to make a lighter version of this wrap gilet, you can work with fewer strands of yarn to create a more open and loose-knit finish to the garment. You can make the garment larger or smaller to suit your own body shape by simply increasing or decreasing the number of stitches cast on and the amount of rows that you work, adjusting yarn amounts accordingly.

hooded scarf

Add a cozy twist to a classic arm knit scarf by creating a simple seamed hood—never again will you have to worry about losing your hat!

materials

- Lion Brand Homespun (98% acrylic, 2% polyester) chunky yarn: 2 x 6 oz (170 g) balls—approx 185 yd (169 m) per ball—of shade 301 Shaker

finished size

Approximate length from top of hood to hem of scarf (one side): 44 in. (112 cm)

time to make

You can make this project in two hours

hooded scarf

Divide the yarn into six equal balls. With six strands held together, draw out three arm lengths for the long-tail cast-on and cast on 7 sts.
Knit 44 rows.
Bind (cast) off.

making up and finishing

Fold in half and align the two short ends. Join the folded section for three rows along one side seam to make the hood and weave in ends. Weave in all remaining yarn tails to finish.

Layer up a selection of short strands of yarn and secure between three longer lengths of yarn. Braid the longer lengths of yarn and knot the shorter ones to create a tassel.

MAKE IT YOURS

For a more chunky or textured design, work in seed (moss) stitch to knit your scarf, and seam as per the instructions above.

multi-wear button scarf

This simple scarf features a selection of oversized statement buttons that allow you to wrap and fasten the scarf in a number of different ways to create a range of different looks to suit your own unique style.

materials

- Debbie Bliss Paloma (60% baby alpaca, 40% merino wool) super chunky yarn:
  2 x 1¾ oz (50 g) balls—approx 71 yd (65 m) per ball—of shade 28 Jade
- Large wooden buttons, four
- Split-eye needle

finished size

Approximate length: 55 in. (140 cm)

time to make

You can make this project in an hour

TIP

You can increase the length of this scarf by adding another skein or two of yarn and continuing to work in the pattern as set. A longer scarf can be wrapped and twisted in even more stylish ways!

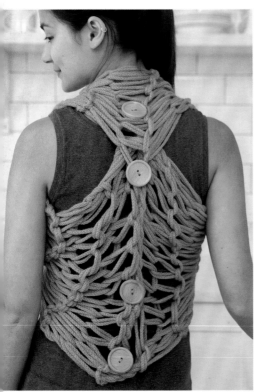

multi-wear button scarf

With the yarn held double (two strands in total), draw out three and a half lengths for the long-tail cast-on and cast on 12 sts.
Row 1: Purl all sts.
Row 2: Knit all sts.
Repeat Rows 1 and 2 ten times more.
Bind (cast) off.

making up and finishing

Weave in all yarn tails. Position the buttons evenly along the bound-off (cast-off) edge and using off-cuts of yarn and the split-eye needle, secure firmly in place to finish.

stylish capelet

This sweet capelet is the perfect feminine finishing touch to drape over your shoulders to beat the chill on cool summer evenings.

materials

- Fyberspates Scrumptious Aran (45% silk, 55% merino wool) worsted yarn:
  3 (**4**, 4) x 3½ oz (100 g) balls—approx 108 yd (165 m) per ball—of shade 408 Rose Pink (A)
- Fyberspates Scrumptious Aran (45% silk, 55% merino wool) worsted yarn:
  1 x 3½ oz (100 g) ball—approx 108 yd (165 m) per ball—of shade 403 Water (B)

finished size

Approximate sizing:
Small—to fit US 2–4 (UK 6–8)
Medium—to fit US 6–8 (UK 10–12)
Large—to fit US 10–12 (UK 14–16)

time to make

You can make this project in an afternoon

fashion capelet

Cape

Divide the skeins of A into four equal balls. With four strands of the yarn held together, draw out six (**seven**, seven) arm lengths and cast on 24 (**26**, 28) sts.

Row 1: Knit all sts.

Row 2: Knit all sts.

Large size only: Knit all sts.

Next row: Decrease row. K2tog (see page 13), knit to last 2 sts, k2tog. [22 (**24**, 26) sts]

Next row: Knit all sts.

Next row: Decrease row. K2tog, knit to last 2 sts, k2tog. [20 (**22**, 24) sts]

Knit next 2 (**3**, 4) rows.

Next row: Decrease row. K2tog, knit to last 2 sts, k2tog. [18 (**20**, 22) sts]

Collar

Row 1: Purl all sts.

Row 2: Purl all sts.

Large size only: Purl all sts.

Bind (cast) off.

> **MAKE IT YOURS**
>
> For a cozier version of this floaty cape, work with a chunkier yarn or add in additional strands of yarn for thicker stitches.

Tie cord

With B held double (two strands in total), finger knit over four fingers (see page 18) until length of knitting measures 86 in. (220 cm) and fasten off (see page 18.)

making up and finishing

Weave in the yarn tails on the tie cord. Weave in the yarn ends on the cape. With the right side uppermost, weave the tie cord neatly back and forth through the stitches along the first row of purl stitches. Fold the collar back over the tie and draw up to fasten around neck.

TIP

The instructions for the different sizes are shown in ascending order: Small (**Medium**, Large). Where there is only one instruction, this applies to all sizes.

fashion cowl

Keep the chill at bay with a cozy arm-knitted cowl—sling it around your neck for effortless style, flip it over your head to create a hood, or loop it around your head for a warm turban effect.

materials

- Lion Brand Homespun (98% acrylic, 2% polyester) chunky yarn: 1 x 6 oz (170 g) ball—approx 185 yd (169 m) per ball—of shade 301 Shaker (A)
- Lion Brand Unique (100% acrylic) chunky yarn: 1 x 6 oz (170 g) ball—approx 109 yd (100 m) per ball—of shade 200 Harvest (B)

finished size

Approximate size: 50 in. (127cm) circumference, 21 in. (53 cm). at its widest point x 25 in. (63.5 cm)

time to make

You can make this project in under an hour

MAKE IT YOURS

Try adding a strand or two of fun fur yarn for a super snuggly and luxurious finish.

fashion cowl

With two strands of A and two strands of B held together (four strands in total), draw out one arm length for the long-tail cast-on and cast on 3 sts.

Rows 1–4: Knit all sts.
Row 5: Kfb, k1, kfb. (5 sts)
Row 6: Knit all sts.
Row 7: Kfb, k3, kfb. (7 sts)
Rows 8–16: Knit all sts.
Row 17: K2tog, k3, k2tog. (5 sts)
Row 18: Knit all sts.
Row 19: K2tog, k1, k2tog. (3 sts)
Rows 20–23: Knit all sts.
Bind (cast) off.

TIP

This pattern is created using increases—knitting into the front and back of a stitch—and decreases—knitting two stitches together. See page 13 for more details of how to do this.

making up and finishing

Fold the knitted strip in half with the right side outermost, align the cast-on and bound-off (cast-off) edges and join together using mattress stitch (see page 20.) Weave in the remaining yarn tails, fasten off, and neatly trim.

quick beanie hat

With only a small amount of yarn you can make your own cozy beanie hat in no time at all!

materials

- Rowan Big Wool (100% merino wool) chunky yarn:
  1 x 3½ oz (100 g) ball—approx 87 yd (80 m) per ball—of shade 061 Concrete (A)

- Rowan Lima Wool (84% baby alpaca, 8% merino wool, 8% nylon) worsted (aran) yarn:
  1 x 1¾ oz (50 g) ball—approx 120 yd (110 m) per ball—of shade 885 Machu Picchu (B)

finished size

Approximate size: circumference 20 in. (50 cm)

time to make

You can make this project in under an hour

TIP

This beanie hat will stretch to fit, but you can always hold the work up to your head while you are knitting to check on the size, and work more rows or stitches if you want to create a larger version.

quick make beanie hat

Holding two strands of A and three strands of B together (five strands in total), draw out one and a half arm lengths for the long-tail cast-on and cast on 7 sts.
Knit 8 rows.
Bind (cast) off.

making up and finishing

Fold the hat in half, aligning the cast-on and bound-off (cast-off) edges. Use the yarn tails to join the two side seams using mattress stitch (see page 20.) Weave in the yarn tails and fasten off. Ease out the knitting at the upper section of the hat to create the beanie shape ready to wear.

MAKE IT YOURS

Mix and match yarn colors for a bright collection of custom beanies.

FINGER KNITS

· ·

for the home

tea-time table set

Variegated yarns create wonderful color patterns when finger knitted into long lengths, folded and stitched; the varying shades make dramatic effects. This soft yet sturdy combo of place mat and coaster will add a bold flourish of color to the dinner table.

materials

- Sirdar Folksong Chunky (51% wool, 49% acrylic) chunky yarn:
  2 x 1¾ oz (50 g) balls—approx 82 yd (75 m) per ball—of shade 377 Pixie Boots
- Needle and sewing thread
- Blocking board or folded towel on an ironing board
- Yarn needle

finished sizes

Place mat, 10 x 8½ in. (25 x 20 cm)
Coaster: 5 x 3½ in. (12 x 9 cm)
One ball of yarn will yield a single table mat, or a set of five coasters.

time to make

You can make this project in a weekend

tea-time table set

Place mat
Finger knit over two fingers (see page 16) until the work measures 404 in. (1028 cm)—using almost the entire ball of yarn.

Coaster:
Finger knit over two fingers until the work measures 72 in. (186 cm).

MAKE IT YOURS
Make larger place mats by joining two balls of yarn and finger knitting longer lengths before pinning out to your chosen size.

making up and finishing

On a blocking board or a folded towel on top of a table, begin laying out the place mat.

Pin a length of finger knitting out to 10 in. (25 cm), without stretching the fabric of the cord too much. Fold the cord back on itself—keeping the stitches straight—and pin the next section of knitting to the same length.

Repeat until the lengths of pinned finger-knitted bands measure 8½ in. (20 cm) wide.

With a needle and sewing thread, begin at one side and start to work through the knitted sections to join them together (see page 20.) Continue to join the sections of finger knitting with lines of stitches up and down the lengths, set 1 in. (2.5 cm) apart.

Once all the strips of finger knitting have been secured, remove the pins to release from the blocking board and weave in the tails of yarn to finish.

TIP

Try to keep the finger knitted sections straight, avoiding twists when stitching. This will help to keep the finished project neat. When sewing strips together, work the stitches through the center of the cords so that they are not visible from the right side of the project.

For the coaster, pin out the length of finger knitting onto the blocking board into 5 in. (12 cm) lengths without stretching the fabric of the cord too much. Fold the cord back on itself—keeping the stitches straight—and pin the next section of knitting to the same length.

Continue folding and pinning until the coaster measures 3½ in. (9 cm) wide. With a needle and sewing thread, begin at one side and start to work through the knitted sections to join them together (see page 20.) Continue to join the sections of finger knitting with lines of stitches up and down the lengths, set 1 in (2.5 cm) apart. After all of the lengths have been secured, remove the pins to release from the blocking board and use a yarn needle to weave in the tails of yarn to finish.

nautical sailor knot pillow

Add a statement piece to your decor with this super-sized nautical sailor knot accent pillow.

materials

- Rowan Tumble (90% alpaca, 10% cotton) super chunky yarn: 2 x 3½ oz (100 g) balls—approx 77 yd (70 m) per ball—of shade 560 Marshmallow (A)

- Katia Big Ribbon (50% cotton, 50% polyester) super chunky yarn: 1 x 7 oz (200 g) ball—approx 77 yd (72 m) per ball—of shade 22 (B)

- Pillow form, 20 in. (50 cm) square

finished size

Approximate size of cover: 21 in. (53 cm) square

time to make

You can make this project in an afternoon

MAKE IT YOURS

Try working with other knot designs to make a set of nautical knot pillows.

nautical sailor knot pillow

Pillow cover

With two strands of A held together, draw out six arm lengths and cast on 16 sts for arm knitting (see page 6).
Arm knit 17 rows (see pages 9–10).
Bind (cast) off.

Nautical accent

With B, finger knit on two fingers (see page 16) until the knitted length measures 125 in. (317.5 cm) or approximately half the ball of yarn.
Fasten off (see page 17.)
Repeat to make one more length of finger-knitted strip in B.

making up and finishing

Pillow cover
Fold the arm-knitted section around the pillow form and use the yarn tails to join the base and side seams with mattress stitch (see page 20.) Knot and weave in the ends.

Nautical sailor knot
Fold both of the finger-knitted strips in half and use them to tie a double-thickness version of the Carrick Bend, shown below.

Pull up the yarn tails and the folded ends of the finger knitting evenly on both sides to tighten the knot.

Position the knot in the center of the pillow front and bring the tails round to the back of the pillow. Weave the lengths of finger knitting through a few of the arm-knitted stitches on the back of the cover to secure them in place, and use the yarn tails of the finger-knitted sections to join them neatly.

TIP

To ensure that you create finger-knitted strips the same length, try re-balling the yarn into two separate, equally sized balls before you begin finger knitting.

1

2

3

spiral bath mat

This simple yet striking bath mat is created by joining together lengths of finger knitting in a spiral. Add some colorful trimmings for a fun finish.

materials

- Katia Cotton Cord (100% cotton) super chunky yarn: 3 x 3½ oz (100 g) balls—approx 55 yd (50 m) per ball—of shade 51 Cream
- Pom pom trimming in contrast color, 2 yd (2 m)
- Needle and sewing thread
- Superglue or hot glue gun
- Printed cotton
- Fusible webbing

finished size

Approximate diameter of mat: 18 in. (46 cm)

time to make

You can make this project in a weekend

MAKE IT YOURS

Work with two colors of finger-knitted lengths and hold them together to create a larger, more colorful spiral.

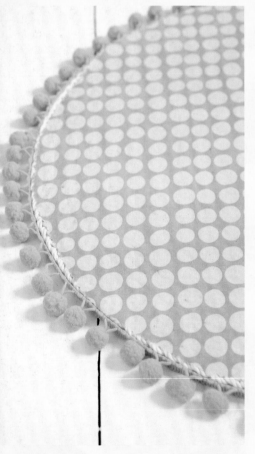

spiral bath mat

Finger knit on two fingers (see page 16) until the work measures 21¾ yd (20 m), using approximately three full balls of yarn and joining in each one with a secure knot in the tails.

Fasten off (see page 17.)

making up and finishing

Starting at the center, begin to coil the length of finger knitting in a spiral. Ensure that you don't pull the knitted cord too tight or the finished mat will curl up. Secure in place with either glue or small hand stitches. Continue working around the spiral until all the knitted cord has been worked into the mat; secure the tail of the cord in place.

Trim the printed cotton and the fusible webbing to the same size as the mat and layer onto the wrong side of the mat with the right side of the printed cotton uppermost and the fusible webbing sandwiched in the middle. Fuse in place with an iron as per the manufacturer's instructions and allow to cool to bond the fabric to the back of the mat.

Work around the outer edge of the mat, pinning the woven tape of the pom pom trim to the last round of finger knitting. Ensure that the pom poms are hanging free, away from the mat. Secure firmly in place with either glue or small neat stitches.

hanging hearts

Create a simple yet stunning hanging decoration in an afternoon, to add a pretty touch to your decor.

materials

- Katia Big Cotton (63% cotton, 37% polyester) chunky yarn:
  1 x 1¾ oz (50 g) ball—approx 27 yd (25 m) per ball—each of shade 51 Cream (A), and shade 52 Lemon (B)
- Ribbon, 35 in. (98 cm)
- Craft wire

finished size

This project is custom-sized to your chosen length

time to make

You can make this project in two hours

> **MAKE IT YOURS**
> Create heart motifs in different sizes or using different yarns to change the finished look of your project.

hanging hearts

With A, finger knit over two fingers (see page 16) until the cord measures 16 in. (40.5 cm) long and fasten off.
Repeat to make one more finger-knitted length in A, and make two more in B.

making up and finishing

Working with each length of finger knitting at a time, use the yarn tails to join the length into a circle. Neatly weave in the yarn tails and fasten off.

Feed a length of craft wire through the piece of finger knitting, keeping it to the center-back of the cord. Join the wire with a small twist and trim, ensuring the ends of the wire are discreetly tucked inside the piece of finger knitting.

Carefully shape the wire into a heart motif.

Repeat to create four finger-knitted heart shapes in total.

Secure one B heart to the bottom of the length of ribbon, by looping the ribbon around the upper center shaping of the heart and neatly knotting. Position an A heart above the lower heart and secure by twisting and then knotting the ribbon around the upper center shaping of the motif. Repeat to add in the next two hearts, following the same color sequence. Once the heart at the top is secured, create a hanging loop by bringing the remaining length of ribbon back to the upper center shaping and tying into a neat bow.

> **TIP**
> When feeding the wire through the section of finger knitting, be sure to work slowly so as not to poke your fingers with the sharp end of the wire. To ensure that the wire is not visible from the front of the work, feed the wire through the center back of the finger-knitted cord.

handy storage tubs

Lengths of finger knitting can be really versatile. This quick and easy make shows you how to transform lashings of finger knitting into colorful custom storage tubs!

materials

- We Are Knitters The Fabric Yarn worsted (aran) weight yarn: 1 x 14 oz (400 g) balls each of shade Yellow (A), Orange (B)
- Needle and sewing thread
- Superglue or hot glue gun

finished size

Approximate size:
Large tub: length 10½ in. (26.5 cm), width 4 in. (10 cm), depth 3½ in. (9 cm)
Small tub: length 8 in. (20 cm), width 4 in. (10 cm), depth 3½ in. (9 cm)

time to make

You can make this project in an afternoon

handy storage tubs

Large tub

With A, finger knit across two fingers (see page 16) until the knitted length measures 7¾ yd (7.1 m)—using approximately one full ball of yarn.
Pass the end of the working yarn through the two remaining loops on the fingers and draw up to create a secure knot in the end of the length of finger knitting.

Small tub

With B, finger knit across two fingers until the knitted length measures 5½ yd. (5 m) using the same technique as for the Large Tub, and fasten off.

making up and finishing

Large tub

Weave in the yarn ends on one end of the finger-knitted strip and lay on a flat surface. Measure 7 in. (17 cm) and fold the strip back on itself, being careful not to twist the strip. At the lower edge bring the finger knitted strip back on itself and lay it along the other side of the initial folded strip. Using small dabs of superglue or hot glue to hold the strips in place, secure together with a needle and matching sewing thread (see page 20.)

Working in the same manner, continue joining the strips until the base of the tub measures 4 in. x 10½ in. (10 cm x 26.5 cm), easing the strip outward at the corners to make a rectangle shape.

TIP

To make the construction of these storage tubs quick and easy, apply dabs of superglue or hot glue to hold sections in place and then secure with stitches. Using a thread that is matched as closely as possible in color to your yarn will help to keep the stitches discreet.

Create the sides of the tub by drawing the knitting strip up onto the outer layer of finger knitting that forms the base; hold in place with small dabs of superglue or hot glue before stitching with a needle and thread to secure firmly in place. Continue working until the sides measure 3½ in. (9 cm) high, ensuring that you finish with the same number of layers the entire way around the tub, and secure in place. Use the remaining yarn tail of the end of the strip to secure the end of the finger knitting in place.

Small tub

Working in the same manner as for the Large Tub, create a base that measures 4 x 8 in. (10 x 20.5 cm) and build the sides in layers, securing with glue then neat hand stitching in matching threads until they measure 3½ in. (9 cm) high. Secure the end of the finger knitting by weaving in the remaining yarn tail.

MAKE IT YOURS
Create different sizes of storage tubs using different lengths of finger knitting, or spiral the finger knitting to create super-sized fabric bowls.

pom pom garland

Pretty garlands are a fantastic way to dress up your home, and make great decorations for parties and celebrations. This colorful design is easy to make!

materials

- Cascade 220 Superwash (100% machine washable merino) worsted yarn:
  1 x 3½oz (100 g) skein—approx 220 yd (200 m) per ball—of shade 871 White (A)
- Aracunia Puelo (100% baby llama) light worsted (DK) yarn:
  1 x 3½ oz (100 g) skein—approx 230 yd (210 m) per skein—of shade 2276 (B)
- Cardboard
- Scissors

finished size

Approximate unstretched size: 76 in (193 cm) long, including hanging ties

time to make

You can make this project in an afternoon

MAKE IT YOURS

You can increase the length of this garland by simply working a longer strip of finger knitting and ensuring that you make enough pom poms to place one every 7 in. (17 cm).

pom pom garland

Garland string

With A and B held together, draw out 10 in. (25 cm) of yarn to create the hanging ties. Place the tail ends of the yarns in the palm of your left hand, leaving the hanging ties below the lower part of your hand. Bring the working yarn over the back of the hand and round the index finger. Finger knit on two fingers (see page 16), holding the two strands together until the finger knitting measures 56 in. (142 cm) in length.
Fasten off (see page 17).
Draw out a further 10 in. (25 cm) of yarn to create the second hanging tie and cut the yarn.

Pom poms

The pom poms are positioned every 7 in. (17 cm) along the length of the garland in alternating colors. For this garland, make five pom poms from A and six from B.

From the cardboard cut two circles, 2 in. (5 cm) in diameter, and then cut out a smaller circle in the center of each. Place the two circles on top of each other and begin winding the yarn around the rings, pushing the yarn through

the central hole and around the outside. Continue wrapping until the cardboard is completely covered. Using the tips of the scissors, carefully cut the yarn around the outer edge by snipping in between the two layers of the cardboard template. Cut a 6 in. (15 cm) length of yarn and wrap this around the center of the pom pom by passing it in between the two halves of the cardboard template. Draw up tightly and knot firmly to secure the strands of the pom pom. Carefully ease the pom pom out of the cardboard template and use the scissors to neaten up any stray strands, leaving the long knotted tails to secure to the garland.

making up and finishing

Start 7 in. (17 cm) in from the cast-on end of the finger-knitted garland string. Use the yarn tails on the pom pom to pass up through the finger knitting and tie securely in place with a knot before trimming away the yarn ends. Repeat to place pom poms every 7 in. (17 cm) along the entire length of the garland string.

FINGER KNITS

· · · · · · · · · · · · · · · · · ·

to wear

TIP

For greater accuracy when splitting the yarns into four separate balls, pop them on a pair of digital kitchen scales to check that the weight of each ball is the same.

See the step-by-step guide on page 18 for finger knitting with three and four fingers.

big bow headband

This quick and easy hair accessory is created from finger-knitted strips. Using a combination of knitting over three and four fingers to create different widths for the knitted pieces, when made up it creates a voluminous, statement bow.

materials

- Louisa Harding Akiko (70% merino wool, 30% alpaca) worsted (aran) weight yarn:
  1 x 1¾ oz (50 g) ball—approx 98 yd (90 m) per ball—of shade 016 Lavender (A)

- Louisa Harding Jesse (100% cotton) worsted (aran) weight yarn:
  1 x 1¾ oz (50 g) ball—approx 97 yd (89 m) per ball—of shade 103 Faded (B)

finished size

Bow is 4¾ in. (12 cm) wide, headband circumference is 19 in. (49 cm)

time to make

You can make this project in under two hours

MAKE IT YOURS

The bow can be secured to a barrette clip or a hair comb if you prefer not to wear a headband, or switch the knitted headband for a length of wide elastic. Substitute silky ribbon yarns for a more glamorous evening look for your hair accessory.

big bow headband

Bow:
With four strands of A held together, finger knit on four fingers (see page 18) until work measures 14 in. (35.5 cm) and fasten off (see page 18.)

Bow center:
With four strands of A held together, knit on three fingers (see page 18) until work measures 4 in. (10 cm) and fasten off (see page 18.)

Headband:
With two strands of A and two strands of B held together (four strands in total), finger knit over four fingers (see page 18) until work measures 19 in. (49 cm). and fasten off (see page 18.)

making up and finishing

Fold the large bow strip in half and use the tails of the yarn to join into a loop and knot to secure.

Fold the loop in half and press flat with the joining seam to the center back of the loop.

Fold the second smaller center strip in half and use the tails of the yarn to join into a loop and knot to secure. Slide over the larger folded section of the bow and position in the center, with the join at the back of the work. Use the tails of the yarn to secure into position in the center before snipping to neaten.

Feed the length of finger knitting for the headband through the back of the small loop at the center of the bow. Use the yarn tails to join the two sections together. Slide the joined section through the center of the bow to hide the join and secure in position with the yarn ends before knotting and snipping to neaten.

layered loop necklace

A single ball of chunky yarn can be transformed into a striking modern necklace with simple finger knitting. By selecting a chunky yarn and finger knitting over two fingers you can create a dense length of knitted cord, which is ideal for making this chunky knitted necklace.

materials

- Katia Big Cotton (63% cotton, 37% nylon) super chunky yarn:
  1 x 1¾ oz (50 g) ball—approx 27 yd (25 m) per ball—of shade 58 (A)
- Drops Alpaca (100% alpaca) fingering (4 ply) yarn:
  1 x 1¾ oz (50 g) ball—approx 182 yd (167 m) per ball—of 2919 Teal (B)
- Needle and sewing thread
- Yarn needle

finished size

Necklace length is 15½ in. (40 cm) at longest point

time to make

You can make this project in under two hours

TIP

See the step-by-step guide on page 16 for finger knitting on two fingers.

layered loop necklace

Cast on in A, knit on two fingers until the work measures 118 in. (300 cm)—using approximately one ball of yarn. Fasten off (see page 17.)

making up and finishing

On a flat surface fold the yarn into a 9½ in. (24 cm) loop. Make a second loop around the first that measures 12 in. (30 cm) and a final loop around the outer part that measures 15½ in. (40 cm).

Position the loops so that the cast-on and bound-off (cast-off) ends of the finger knitting meet at one side of the necklace and the three bands lay flat against each other.

Use the yarn tails from the cast-on and fastened-off ends of the knitted length to weave through the sections to join into a loop.

With a needle and sewing thread work a few stitches through the finger knitting to secure the joined ends into place. With the needle and thread work through the upper 15½ in. (40 cm) of the necklace to hold the three lengths flat together—this will form the back of the necklace.

Thread B onto a yarn needle and secure onto the joined section with a small stitch through the finger-knitted sections and knot the yarn. Begin wrapping the yarn over the joined section, continue wrapping until 3 in. (7.5 cm) is covered with a band of wrapped yarn.

Once the section is fully covered, thread B onto the yarn needle and secure through to the necklace with a small, discreet knot to finish.

MAKE IT YOURS

Switch the fingering (4 ply) yarn to a different shade to suit your style, wrap with a length of leather thong, or stitch a band of pretty print cotton in place of the yarn binding, and secure with hand stitches.

floral corsage brooch

This quick and easy finger-knitted accessory can be made with small amounts of yarn—make it this afternoon and wear it tonight!

materials

- Cascade 220 (100% Peruvian highland wool) worsted (aran) yarn: 1 x 3½ oz (100 g) ball—approx 220 yd (200 m) per ball— each of shade 9463 Gold (A), shade 8863 Mellow Mauve (B), and shade 8951 Aqua (C)
- Yarn needle
- Brooch back

finished size

Approximate size:
flower measures 6 in. (15 cm) across

time to make

You can make this project in under two hours

floral corsage brooch

Bloom center

With A, finger knit across two fingers (see page 16), until the knitted length measures 4 in. (10 cm).
Fasten off (see page 17.)
Repeat to make two more 4 in. (10 cm) lengths of finger-knitted strips in A.

Flower petals

With B, finger knit across two fingers to create three lengths of finger knitting measuring 35 in. (89 cm) each.
With C, finger knit across two fingers to create one length of finger knitting measuring 25 in. (63 cm) each.

> **MAKE IT YOURS**
> Add a touch of glamour to the corsage by sewing on a selection of beads or buttons to the middle of the finished bloom.

making up and finishing

Use the yarn tails to knot the three 4 in. (10 cm) finger knitted strips (Yarn A) together at one end. Braid (plait) the strips and secure the braid in place by knotting neatly with the remaining yarn tails. Fold the braided strip into a neat spiral. Working on the wrong side, use the yarn tails to weave through the sections to secure the spiral in place.

Use the yarn tails to knot the three 35 in. (89 cm) strips in B together at one end. Braid the strips and secure the braid in place by knotting neatly with the remaining yarn tails.

Fold the braided strip into five even petals and, using the yarn needle and yarn tail, secure in place with neat stitches through the center. Weave in the remaining yarn ends and knot before trimming neatly.

Fold the finger-knitted strip in C into five petal shapes and use the yarn needle and yarn tail to secure the loops in place. Position on top of the braided bloom section in B, and use the yarn tails and yarn needle to secure into place. Weave in the ends and knot before snipping neatly.

Position the bloom center (in A) on top of the middle of the flower and using the yarn tails and the yarn needle, secure neatly in place with a few stitches, ensuring they work through all the layers of the flower for a secure finish. Position the brooch back centrally on the reverse of the corsage and fasten in place, use the yarn tails to work several stitches around the back of the brooch clasp. Weave in the ends and knot before snipping neatly.

TIP

This project uses only small quantities of yarn—you will be able to make a large number of these corsages from a single skein of each color, making them great gifts— or alternatively, you can work with worsted (aran) weight yarns from your stash!

color-block clutch purse

Team two bold shades of light worsted (DK) yarn to make striking and colorful strips of finger knitting, creating your own stylish clutch purse.

materials

- Sublime Extra Fine Merino Wool DK (100% extra fine merino wool) light worsted (DK) yarn:
  2 x 1¾ oz (50 g) balls—approx 127 yd (116 m) per ball—of shade 361 Gem (A)
  1 x 1¾ oz (50g) ball—approx 127 yd (116 m) per ball—of shade 349 Sunday (B)
- Needle and matching sewing thread
- Superglue or hot glue gun
- Large button

time to make

You can make this project in an afternoon

finished size

Approximate size:
Width—12 in. (30 cm)
Height—5½ in. (14 cm)
Depth—3 in. (7.5 cm)

color-block clutch purse

With A, finger knit over two fingers (see page 16) until the knitted length measures 15¾ yd (14.5 m)—using approximately two full balls of yarn.
Fasten off (see page 17.)
Using the same technique working over two fingers, use B to create a finger-knitted strip measuring 85 in. (216 cm) and fasten off.

MAKE IT YOURS

To create a larger purse, opt for a chunkier yarn to make your finger-knitted strips.

making up and finishing

Weave in the yarn ends on one end of the knitted strip in A and lay on a flat surface. Measure 9½ in. (24 cm) and fold the strip back on itself, being careful not to twist the strip. At the lower edge bring the finger-knitted strip back on itself and lay it along the other side of the initial folded strip. Use small dabs of superglue or hot glue to hold the strips in place, then stitch through with a needle and matching thread to secure together. Working in the same manner, continue joining the strips until the base of the purse measures 12 in. (30 cm) x 3 in. (7.5 cm), easing the strip around the ends to create an elongated oval base.

Create the sides of the purse by drawing the knitted strip up onto the outer layer of finger knitting that forms the base. Hold in place with small dabs of superglue or hot glue before stitching with a needle and thread to secure. Continue working around the sides until they measure 4½ in. (11.5 cm) high, ensuring that you finish with the same number of layers the entire way around the purse. Join in the strip of finger knitting in B. Using the same technique to secure the finger knitting, work three more layers around the upper section of the purse, ending at the center back, leaving 9 in. (23 cm) of knitting unsecured for the fastening.

Position the large button on the center front of the purse and secure in place with neat hand stitches using the needle and sewing thread.

Fold the unsecured length of finger knitting back to create a fastening loop and use the yarn tails to secure firmly into position at the base of the loop to finish.

TIP

Using small dabs of glue to secure the lengths of finger-knitted cord in place as you create the purse will not only make the process of joining the strips together easier, but will help to give the bag added structure.

stack 'em up bangles

This trio of colorful fabric yarn bracelets are great statement accessories—finger knitting over two, three, and four fingers gives you bangles of different widths.

materials

- We Are Knitters The Fabric Yarn worsted (aran) weight yarn: Small quantities of Lime Green (A), Turquoise (B), and Pink(C)

finished size

Approximate size: internal circumference 7 in. (17 cm)

time to make

You can make this project in an hour

TIP

Fabric yarn can be quite stretchy, so be sure to measure the strip against your wrist—it will need to be a snug fit so that the bangle does not slip off.

stack 'em up bangles

Skinny bangle

With A, finger knit across two fingers (see page 16) until the length measures 9 in. (22.5 cm) or the length required to fit snugly around your wrist.
Pass the end of the working yarn through the two remaining loops on the fingers and draw up to create a secure knot in the end of the length of finger knitting.

Midi bangle

With B, finger knit across three fingers (see page 18) until the knitted length measures 9 in. (22.5 cm) or the length required to fit snugly around your wrist.
Pass the end of the working yarn through the two remaining loops on the fingers and draw up to create a secure knot in the end of the length of finger knitting.

Chunky Bangle

With C, finger knit across four fingers (see page 18) until the knitted length measures 9 in. (22.5 cm) or the length required to fit snugly around your wrist.
Pass the end of the working yarn through the two remaining loops on the fingers and draw up to create a secure knot in the end of the length of finger knitting.

making up and finishing

Use the cast-on and fastened-off tails of yarn to join the finger-knitted strips into circles by passing each tail through the opposite end in turn and knotting securely. Repeat to join all three strips into bangles. Snip the yarn tails and weave the ends inside the strip to finish.

MAKE IT YOURS

You can make these bangles a custom-fit by finger-knitting either longer or shorter strips. Measure the strips against your wrist as you work to get the perfect size for you.

beaded leather necklace

Finger knitting with a thin leather cord and combining with
a selection of glass beads is a great way to create an
accessory that is really striking.

materials

- Leather thong 1 mm gauge, 2½ yd (2.2 m) long, natural tan
- Selection of glass beads in a range of colors, shapes, and sizes

finished size

Approximate size: the necklace has a sliding knot closure and can be worn long or short, to suit your style

time to make

You can make this project in an afternoon

beaded leather necklace

On a flat surface, lay out your chosen beads. You can either
place these in a symmetrical design or you can add them
randomly for a more eclectic finish. Tie a large loose knot
into the end of the leather thong: this will prevent the
beads falling off. Begin to slide the selection of beads onto
the thong in your desired order.

Once the beads have been threaded on, draw out a 14 in.
(35.5 cm) tail of leather thong which will become the length
and fastening.

With the tail end of the leather thong, finger knit over two
fingers (see page 16.) As you work, slide one bead at a
time up the length and into the section making the stitch.
Continue to make the stitch, working the leather thong
around the bead to secure it into place. As you continue to
make the stitches, randomly slide the next bead on the
leather thong up into the working stitch to secure it.
Continue finger knitting in this manner adding in all the
beads until the knitted length measures 8 in. (20 cm) —
leaving a 14 in. (35 cm) tail of leather thong at the end
which will become the second part of the length and
fastening.

Pass the end of the leather thong through the two
remaining loops on the fingers and draw up to create a
secure knot in the end of the length of finger knitting.

MAKE IT YOURS

This necklace looks great worked with lots of large
statement beads. If you want a more subtle look, simply
select smaller beads or use only one style or color.

making up and finishing

The finger knitted-beaded section will be positioned in the
center of the leather thong. Place on a flat surface and
draw the ends up to make a circle, overlapping at each end
so that the cut ends of the leather thong sit level with the
end of the beaded section on the opposite side. Working
on each side in turn, fold a 3 in. (7.5 cm) loop. With the end
of the leather thong make three tight wraps around the
leather working down toward the looped end. Ensure that
the leather is wrapped tightly around both parts of the loop
and the part that leads to the necklace. Feed the tail of the
thong though the loop and draw up tightly to secure. This
will create a neat knot that can slide back and forth along
the length of leather. Repeat to create an identical knot on
the second side of the necklace and trim away the ends of
the leather thong protruding from each knot to neaten.
Slide the two knots together to lengthen the necklace to
put it on and adjust to your desired length for wearing by
sliding the two knots apart to shorten.

linked up scarf

Create a clever springtime accessory by joining neat finger-knitted strips to make a chain link scarf.

materials

- Sublime Extra Fine Merino Wool DK (100% extra fine merino wool) light worsted (DK) yarn:
  1 x 1¾ oz (50 g) ball—approx 127 yd (116 m) per ball—each of shade 373 Pumpkin (A), and shade 362 Spruce (B)

- Yarn needle

finished size

Approximate size:
length: 75 in. (190 cm)

time to make

You can make this project in an afternoon

TIP

For a really neat finish ensure that the finger-knitted strips are exactly the same length, as this will create more uniform links in the chain.

linked up scarf

With two strands of A held together, finger knit over two fingers (see page 16) until the knitted length measures 8 in. (20 cm).
Fasten off (see page 17.)
Repeat to make 14 more 8 in. (20 cm) lengths of finger-knitted strips in A—15 strips in total.
With two strands of B held together, work in the same manner to create three 8 in. (20 cm) lengths of finger-knitted strips.

making up and finishing

With a strip of finger knitting in A, fold into a circle aligning the two ends to make a loop. Use the yarn tails to join them together with a couple of neat stitches. Knot the yarn and weave in before trimming. Place a second strip of finger-knitting in A through the loop just created and join in the same manner; this will create the line of the chain. Repeat to join ten more strips in A in the same manner to make a length of chain with 12 links in A. Add three links of B, and finish with three links of A.

MAKE IT YOURS

Create a two-tone version of this scarf by working with one strand of each color held together to create each finger-knitted link.

suppliers

The projects featured in this book have been created using a selection of wonderful yarns—here are some online suppliers to get you started on your arm and finger knitting journey.

yarns

Aracunia
www.knittingfever.com
www.designeryarns.uk.com

Cascade 220
www.cascadeyarns.com
www.loveknitting.com

Debbie Bliss
www.designeryarns.uk.com
www.knittingfever.com

Fyberspates
www.fyberspates.co.uk
www.fyberspatesusa.com

Hoooked Zpaghetti
www.dmccreative.co.uk
www.hoooked.nl/uk

Katia
www.katia.com
www.knittingfever.com

Lion Brand
www.lionbrand.com
www.deramores.com

Louisa Harding
www.knittingfever.com
www.designeryarns.uk.com

Rowan
www.knitrowan.com
www.jimmybeanswool.com

Sirdar
www.sirdar.co.uk
www.knittingfever.com

Sublime
www.sublimeyarns.com
www.knittingfever.com

We Are Knitters
www.weareknitters.com

non-yarn supplies

Ikea
www.ikea.com

Fusible webbing
www.vilene-retail.com

index

acknowledgments

Working on such a creative and inspired book as this has been an exciting challenge. There have been so many people who have contributed to the coming together of this collection of no-needle makes.

First, endless thanks to my husband, John Strutt, for his artistic flair, problem solving and unfaltering support. A special thank you to Anne Styles, my mum, for teaching me to love knitting (with needles!) and giving me such a strong creative foundation.

Thank you to the companies that have supplies the incredible yarns for this book: Lion Brand, We Are Knitters, Katia Yarns, DMC, Designer Yarns, Cascade Yarns, Fyberstates, and Rowan.

Finally a huge thank you to Cindy Richards and Penny Craig at CICO Books for commissioning such a fantastic, modern, and fun knitting book, and for their support and enthusiasm throughout—this has been a real joy to work on!

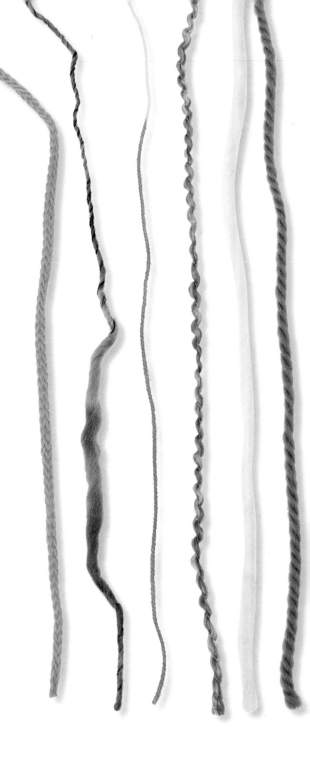